W9-BYK-046

HOW MONEY WORKS

WORLD MONEY

By Gerry Bailey
and Felicia Law

Illustrated by Mark Beech

NORWOOD HOUSE PRESS
Chicago, Illinois

NORWOOD HOUSE  PRESS

P.O. Box 316598 · Chicago, Illinois 60631
For more information about Norwood House Press please visit our website at
www.norwoodhousepress.com or call 866-565-2900.

LIBRARY OF CONGRESS CATALOGING-IN-PUBLICATION DATA

Bailey, Gerry, 1945-
 World money / written by Gerry Bailey and Felicia Law.
   pages cm. -- (How money works)
 Illustrated by Mark Beech.
 Includes index.
 Summary: "Presents an introduction to financial literacy and the global economy, discussing how
countries trade, value their currency, and manage poverty and wealth. Includes index, glossary, and
discussion questions"-- Provided by publisher.
 ISBN 978-1-59953-720-7 (library edition : alk. paper) -- ISBN 978-1-60357-823-3 (ebook)
 1. Money--Juvenile literature. 2. Foreign exchange--Juvenile literature. 3. Finance--Juvenile literature.
 4. Economics--Juvenile literature. I. Law, Felicia. II. Beech, Mark, 1971- illustrator. III. Title.
 HG221.5.B2573 2015
 332.4--dc23
            2015003635

274N – 062015
Manufactured in the United States of America in North Mankato, Minnesota.

WORLD MONEY

HOW THE WORLD SPENDS
ITS MONEY – AND WHY

Contents

Words that appear in red throughout the text are defined in the glossary on pages 62-63.

The World and Its Money

WHO NEEDS MONEY?

Everyone in the world uses money. It may look different in different countries, and it may have different names and entirely different values, but it will all work as money. And that's because each government decides what money can be legally used.

We all agree

Everyone who uses money – and as we know, that's everybody – accepts certain things about what money is:

* It's a unit for adding up the value of wealth.
* It's something you can exchange for stuff. You can buy and sell with it.
* It can be considered "goods." You can buy and sell units of money just as you'd buy or sell coffee.
* You can reward people, give it away as a present, do what you like with it …

… but everyone accepts that it has a value.

DAY t⊛ DAY

Everyone agrees about the value of their money when buying things. Generally, the value, or purchasing power, of each coin and each bill doesn't change much from day to day. A dollar is a dollar and it buys more or less the same amount of something from one day to the next.

Of course, if something dramatic happens in a country, such as a war, the value of the coins and bills may suddenly change. Maybe food is short so you have to use more coins to buy a bag of rice than you did before. It doesn't always take a major event for this to happen!

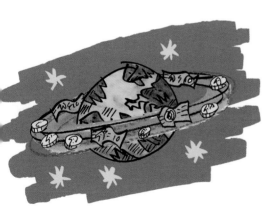

TRUSTiNG m⊛NEY

So, we all have our own kind of money. And we trust it, and use it, and accept that it has a certain value. But do we trust and use each other's money? And why should we need to?

Well, there may be thousands of miles lying between us, but when it comes to trade, we generally need another country's money in order to pay for the stuff we buy in that country.

All m⊛NEY iS REAllY W⊛RID m⊛NEY.

Money Has History

There's nothing new about world money.
This is because there's nothing new about trade.
Countries have been trading with each other for
thousands of years, and that meant constantly
swapping one kind of money for another as
traders traveled about and bought and sold goods.

Barter

Swapping, or barter as it's known, is a good way
for two people to get the things they want from
each other.

From the point where early man settled in one
place and grew crops, he often found he had too
much of the things he'd grown, and too little of
the things he hadn't. He needed to exchange
his surplus goods for something he didn't have
but needed. And this meant going to market
and making a trade.

The earliest trade was just this – swapping one
set of goods for another. Of course, both buyer and
seller had to agree on a value for their goods – and
both had to want what the other one had – which
wasn't always easy.

BEYOND the Village

At first, people bartered goods with the next village or tribe, but as they began to make more and more of necessities such as pots and cloth, and luxuries such as jewelry and wine, traders traveled further and further to exchange goods. And as trade grew and barter became complicated, a better way was needed.

COINS take OVER

Eventually, money in the form of coins, and later notes, was introduced as the 'medium of exchange.' This meant that money became an accepted alternative to goods and had a value of its own. In other words, goods could now be 'swapped' or traded for money.

PACIFY bY COIN

Actually, coins were in use long before they replaced barter. Although they weren't used in trade, they were used to keep the enemy quiet. The verb 'to pay' comes from the Latin word "pacare," which originally meant to pacify, or make peace with. If a tribe wanted to make peace with another, it had to 'pay' for that peace by using a 'unit of value' acceptable to both sides.

And early coins were used to do this.

Across the Seas

Over time, trade began to open up the world. Traders were able to cross oceans and continents and establish trade routes that crisscrossed the globe. Trade between countries began to expand.

The new merchants

Throughout the 1500s and 1600s, trade opened up both over land and across oceans, with great ports developing to become bustling merchant centers.

With foreign trade came a new group of merchants and adventurers. Merchants were exchanging goods for materials they didn't have locally. They sold goods to rich people, goods they had probably never seen before, and became rich themselves.

Back and Forth

In 1271, Marco Polo left Venice with his father and uncle to travel east toward China and the cities of the great Kublai Khan. They traveled the ancient 'silk road' to get there and stayed for 24 years. The Polos showed that trade between faraway countries was possible and profitable.

• • • • • • • • • • • • • • • •

In the 1400s, European sea explorers like Columbus, Vasco da Gama, and later Magellan, set sail toward the east and then the west, to discover new lands and new trading possibilities.

• • • • • • • • • • • • • • • •

Traveling in the opposite direction, the Chinese admiral Zheng He set off in ships with the most basic of charts and maps and nautical equipment. His was the largest fleet of ships ever recorded.

Exotic trade

They all hoped to discover new rich countries where they could gather up exotic local products – from tobacco, olive oil, and spices, to gold and glassware, the scent frankincense, and exotic animals such as monkeys.

Goods for sale

foreign foods

oils and scents

exotic animals

gold and precious jewels

All these goods were new and exciting to the people back home.

11

BUSY SEAS

It's easy to take for granted the silk clothes we buy that were made in China and Thailand, the tea we drink from India, the olives flown in from Spain, or the family car that was made in Japan. International trade is familiar to us all today.

Great trading ports

As trade grew, so did the world's great ports. Singapore became a link between east and west. European ports such as Genoa in Italy, Lisbon in Portugal, and London in England became stepping-off points for exploration as well as centers of trade and business.

Today, almost every country with a coastline or large river that enters the sea, has a large port.

Container ships

The goods are mostly brought across the seas on huge container ships. Containers can be piled high and make carrying goods much easier. A loaded container can simply be put onto a ship, truck, or train without having to be emptied.

Great ports
Shanghai CHINA
Singapore SINGAPORE
Hong Kong CHINA
Busan SOUTH KOREA
Dubai UAE
Rotterdam NETHERLANDS
Kaohsiung TAIWAN
Hamburg GERMANY
Los Angeles U.S.

Money links us

Modern trade couldn't happen without money. So money holds us all together – working, spending, saving, traveling … In fact, money is the link between you and thousands of other people – absolute strangers – all of whom affect your life!

Let's find out how this can be.

World Money

The fact is that money wasn't just invented in one place. It developed in all kinds of ways and in many different parts of the world. It started in one form and changed as country after country passed it around.

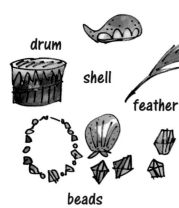

drum

shell

feather

beads

An early Roman coin

Very early coins from Greece and Japan

valuable coins

It was only a matter of time before bits of silver and gold took over as a common exchange. Precious metals were chosen because they were valuable in their own right. They could act as a standard measure of value, so everyone would know how much an ox or duck was worth in gold coins.

Bits and bobs

All sorts of crazy forms of money have cropped up in the past – amber, beads, cowrie shells, drums, eggs, feathers, to name just a few.

Notes

Bills started out in Europe as receipts that people received when they deposited gold in the vaults of goldsmiths. The receipt was a promise to pay out the amount in gold when it was presented. These receipts soon became money in their own right and eventually, the notes we use today.

Money words

Currency
A generally accepted form of money, including bills and coins, issued by a government.

Denomination
Coins like the euro, Swiss franc, and Australian dollar are some of hundreds of different world currencies. The value of the coin or bill is printed clearly on it. This is known as its denomination.

Face value
This is an expression often used to emphasize that the value printed on the bill or coin can be trusted.

Legal tender
This describes all the different denominations of a country's currency that have been adopted by that country's government for general use.

Bills from top:
* Nepal
* Malaysia
* Egypt
* U.S.
* Europe

WORLD CURRENCIES

Afghanistan

Here are just some countries and the names of their currencies:

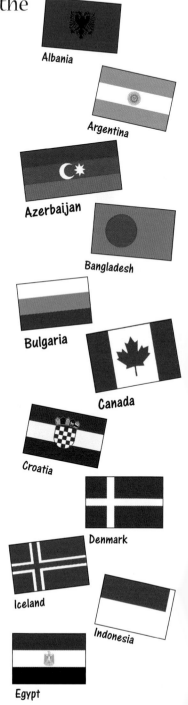

Afghanistan	**Afghan** afghani
Albania	**Albanian** lek
Algeria	**Algerian** dinar
Argentina	**Argentine** peso
Australia	**Australian** dollar
Azerbaijan	**Azerbaijani** manat
Bangladesh	**Bangladeshi** taka
Bhutan	**Bhutanese** ngultrum
Brazil	**Brazilian** real
Bulgaria	**Bulgarian** lev
Canada	**Canadian** dollar
Chile	**Chilean** peso
China, People's Republic of	**Chinese** yuan renminbi
Croatia	**Croatian** kuna
Czech Republic	**Czech** koruna
Denmark	**Danish** krone
Egypt	**Egyptian** pound
Hungary	**Hungarian** forint
Iceland	**Icelandic** króna
India	**Indian** rupee
Indonesia	**Indonesian** rupiah

Iraq

Japan

South Africa

New Zealand

Pakistan

Peru

Philippines

Switzerland

Turkey

Ukraine

United Kingdom

Iran	**Iranian rial**
Iraq	**Iraqi dinar**
Japan	**Japanese yen**
Korea, South	**South Korean won**
Malaysia	**Malaysian ringgit**
Mexico	**Mexican peso**
Morocco	**Moroccan dirham**
New Zealand	**New Zealand dollar**
Norway	**Norwegian kroner**
Pakistan	**Pakistani rupee**
Peru	**Peruvian nuevo sol**
Philippines	**Philippine peso**
Romania	**Romanian leu**
Russia	**Russian ruble**
Saudi Arabia	**Saudi riyal**
South Africa	**South African rand**
Sweden	**Swedish krona**
Switzerland	**Swiss franc**
Taiwan New	**Taiwan dollar**
Thailand	**Thai baht**
Turkey	**Turkish lira**
Ukraine	**Ukrainian hryvnia**
United Kingdom	**British pound**
United States	**United States dollar**
Vietnam	**Vietnamese dong**

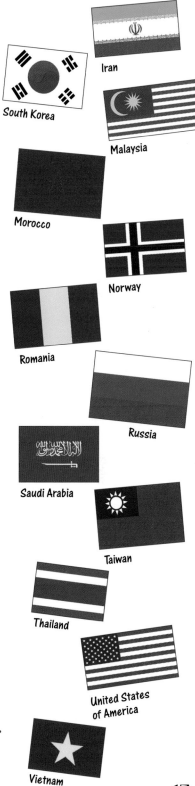

Iran

South Korea

Malaysia

Morocco

Norway

Romania

Russia

Saudi Arabia

Taiwan

Thailand

United States of America

Vietnam

Foreign Exchange

It would be much easier if every country in the world had developed the same kind of coins and bills – we'd all be using a 'worldthalar' as the early science-fiction writers used to call it. But, as we know, every country has its own kind of money. And even when they call it by the same name, such as 'cent,' it doesn't mean the actual value will be the same.

BUYING CURRENCIES

If you're going on vacation to a foreign country, you'll need to buy foreign currency. For instance, if you're going to France you'll need euros, if you're going to the U.S. you'll need dollars, and if you're going to China you'll need yuan.

You can buy foreign currency at a bank – most banks have a foreign currency counter, where you can buy almost any currency. The bank probably won't carry Albanian lek or Colombian pesos, but it will carry euros, dollars, or pounds. There will be a fee for making the exchange, which might be a small percentage of the total with a minimum amount for each separate transaction.

foreign money

What happens when you come across a coin, bank note, or bill that's been issued in a different country? Is it still money?
Yes, it certainly is, because it can buy things in the country in which it was issued. It can also be used to buy other currencies.

So, if you were given Japanese yen, for example, you could use them to buy pounds or dollars or any other currency. This is called currency exchange.

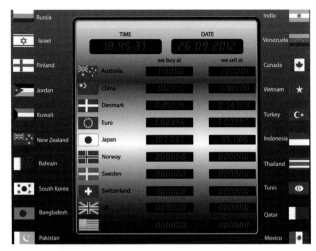

Exchange boards show rates to buy and rates to sell for all the main currencies.

You can often change money at good rates in a local exchange shop.

rate of exchange

You might get a better rate of exchange at a bank or online than in a currency exchange shop. But be aware that exchange rates are different when you buy compared to when you sell. You'll always get a better rate when you buy. Money changers usually give both rates. So, it's best to get rid of all your foreign money before you return home.

CURRENCY EXCHANGE

When countries want to trade with each other, they mostly want to buy and sell using their own currency. So before international trading can take place, it has to be possible to trade currencies. For instance, if you wanted to buy lanterns from China, you'd have to pay in Chinese yuan. This means you'd have to be able to buy yuan with your pounds, dollars, or pesos.

USE the DOllaR

Today, many countries set, or peg, the value of their money to the value of the U.S. dollar, so this makes it easier. It's called a fixed exchange rate. This is how it works …

Each country decides how much of their currency is worth 1 U.S. dollar. It might look something like this: 1 Chinese yuan = 0.16 U.S. dollar. This means you would need more than 6 Chinese yuan to buy a U.S. dollar.

So if a Chinese lantern costs 1 Chinese yuan, you will get 6 of them – and some change – when you offer the seller 1 dollar.

Sometimes, trade is made easier when traders agree to work in one currency, such as the dollar.

Floating Exchange Rate

Some currencies are said to 'float.' This means that the exchange rate value of a currency will change from day to day. The value of the currency depends upon supply and demand in the market. Some currencies are popular and people want to buy them or invest in them. Their value is high. Some are less popular and their value is low.

Buying and Selling Currencies

Each day, currency exchange rates are listed for everyone around the world to see. Banks and money changers, in fact everyone who works with money, all watch these lists carefully so they can swap currencies at the right rate.

Currencies are bought and sold just like goods such as wheat or oil. The money traders who do this work need to be alert, as the value of a currency can change from minute to minute.

If you buy 1,000 dollars in the morning, it may cost you more than if you buy them that afternoon.

Trade

Most of what countries do with the money they earn involves buying and selling. Buying and selling is all about trade – using money to buy the things they need, and selling to people the things that they need. Trade is what keeps the money moving around.

• • • • • • • • • • • • • • • • • • •

A trade = an agreement

Because trade involves an exchange of goods that makes both the seller and the buyer happy, trade always involves an agreement or a deal. The final deal is absolute. You meet, you make a deal, you walk away. That's what trade is all about.

Specialization

Thousands of years ago, when people first settled into villages and started farming, they got rid of their extra products by trading with other villages. At the same time, some villages became better at doing certain things than others – making arrowheads or woolly mammoth pendants This is called specialization, and it creates an even bigger demand for trade.

international trade

Today, the same thing applies on a far bigger scale. Countries, or nations, tend to concentrate on producing goods and services where they have a natural advantage over other countries.

Let's say there were only two countries: Saudi Arabia and Jamaica. Saudi Arabia produces more oil than it can possibly use. But it can't grow sugar cane, and everyone wants sugar. Jamaica can grow loads of sugar cane because it has the right climate, but it needs oil for gas, fuel, and so on.

Providing there are no barriers to trading, Saudi Arabia can trade oil to Jamaica, while Jamaica can trade sugar to Saudi Arabia. They can exchange commodities, the products they have most access to.

An oil refinery lit up at night.

A sugar cane plantation in Jamaica.

This kind of specialization in trade allows countries to sell goods and earn money to buy materials they may not be able to grow or find themselves.

it is called international trade.

IMPORT - EXPORT

BUYiNG FROM each other

Goods and services that are brought into a country to sell are called imports. Imports cost nations money because the company that imports them has to pay for them. So, money moves out of the country.

Countries import goods or services because they cannot produce them for themselves and they're necessary, or because they're cheaper to buy abroad than to manufacture at home.

QUOTAS

Some imports have restrictions applied to them, such as an import tax, known as 'duty.' Often, a certain amount of an item can be brought into a country. This is called a quota.

Let's say lots of workers in your country earn their living by making cars. If too many cheaper, foreign cars were allowed in, fewer local cars might be bought, and workers would lose their jobs. This kind of protection is sometimes necessary.

Selling to each other

Exports are goods and services that are supplied to and bought by companies or governments in other countries. Exporting, or selling lots of goods abroad, is good for a country because it brings cash in and creates wealth.

Money earned from exports benefits a country's wealth. Exports are usually paid for in the currency of the supplier. They may be goods and services that a country can produce easily or that are wanted by countries abroad.

For example, the United States has large areas of land that are just right for wheat growing. So it exports wheat to countries that cannot grow wheat for themselves.

eBay

eBay is just one of many new ways that people across the world now trade with each other. They don't need to meet to do a deal – they do it online.

eBay is the largest online trading market in the world. Imagine over 100 million people all buying and selling to each other! It's just like a local street market – but in cyberspace. People not only buy and sell on this global auction site, but they chat and argue too, just like they did in the old marketplaces hundreds of years ago.

As well as professional eBay sellers, millions of people add to their income by selling stuff on eBay.

GETTING A BALANCE

Sometimes you hear a newscaster telling you that the trade balance of the country is 'up or down.' The figures they give out are in millions of dollars, or even billions. You may wonder who's doing all this trading and why so much money is involved. Well, it's less complicated than you might think.

Keeping a balance

A country's trade balance is about what the country has sold abroad and what it has bought from abroad.

Most countries try to find a balance between their exports and their imports, so when they export a great deal, they also tend to import a great deal as well.

Together, all the money that flows in and out of a country makes up its economy.

Canada

Germany
UK
France
Italy
Netherlands

U.S.

The trade gap

When the value of what a country buys exceeds what it sells, it has a trade gap.

The balance ✹f payments

A balance of payments is a record used by governments to keep count of the money flowing into a country and the money flowing out. Keeping this type of record makes it possible for nations to determine if the current balance between imports and exports is acceptable, or if they need to take steps to change the balance. This record is kept year by year.

Top importers
* United States
* Germany
* United Kingdom
* France
* Japan
* China
* Italy
* Canada
* Hong Kong
* Netherlands

Top exporters
* China
* United States
* Germany
* Japan
* France
* South Korea
* Netherlands
* Russia
* Italy
* United Kingdom

Germany
UK
France
Italy
Netherlands

Russia

China

Japan

South Korea

Hong Kong

Who sells what?

These are the ten countries that sell the most goods around the world – and what they sell.

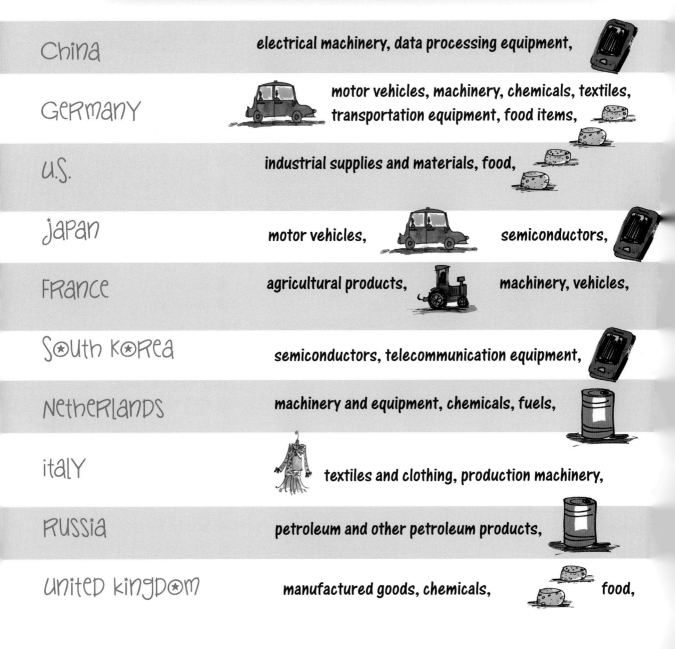

China	electrical machinery, data processing equipment,
Germany	motor vehicles, machinery, chemicals, textiles, transportation equipment, food items,
U.S.	industrial supplies and materials, food,
Japan	motor vehicles, semiconductors,
France	agricultural products, machinery, vehicles,
South Korea	semiconductors, telecommunication equipment,
Netherlands	machinery and equipment, chemicals, fuels,
Italy	textiles and clothing, production machinery,
Russia	petroleum and other petroleum products,
United Kingdom	manufactured goods, chemicals, food,

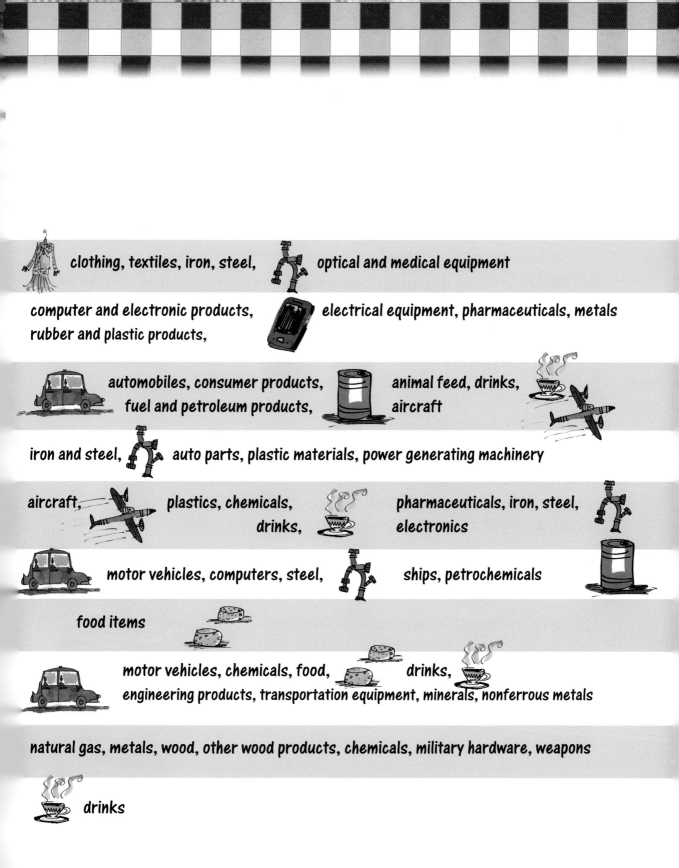

clothing, textiles, iron, steel, optical and medical equipment

computer and electronic products, electrical equipment, pharmaceuticals, metals
rubber and plastic products,

automobiles, consumer products, animal feed, drinks,
fuel and petroleum products, aircraft

iron and steel, auto parts, plastic materials, power generating machinery

aircraft, plastics, chemicals, pharmaceuticals, iron, steel,
drinks, electronics

motor vehicles, computers, steel, ships, petrochemicals

food items

motor vehicles, chemicals, food, drinks,
engineering products, transportation equipment, minerals, nonferrous metals

natural gas, metals, wood, other wood products, chemicals, military hardware, weapons

drinks

WORLD BRANDS

A brand can be a product, a group of products, or a company. But it's more than that. It's a name and an association. It's what sticks in your mind when you think of a product or group of products. It is usually a very valuable asset, as people are willing to pay more for products from a company with a strong brand.

WORLD brands

Coca-Cola is probably the brand people around the world recognize most. It means that when you think of a brown, sweet, fizzy drink that makes you feel good, the first words that come into your mind are Coca-Cola. Nike is another brand name that is instantly recognizable.

But a brand is also a promise. Almost every owner of a famous brand has tried hard to establish a set of values that consumers will like and understand. Owners want their brand to represent something trustworthy and honest.

Brands can become global and the products they represent can be sold anywhere in the world they are wanted.

Apple is famous for its computers and software.

Coca-Cola is a universal drink.

Nike has stores that sell its gear worldwide.

McDonald's is a favorite fast-food restaurant.

T★P bRANDS?

Each year people are questioned about what they think are the best brands. Here are some answers:

✳ Gap	✳ Apple
✳ Disney	✳ Nike
✳ McDonald's	✳ Coca-Cola
✳ KFC	✳ Starbucks

GETTING ACROSS BORDERS

In today's high-tech world of international trade, most buying and selling of goods between countries is carried out over the phone, over the Internet, or through a bank using a Bill of Exchange.

Bill of exchange

A Bill of Exchange is a written, unconditional order by one party (the drawer) to another (the drawee) to pay a certain sum, either immediately or on a fixed date, for payment of goods and/or services received. The drawee accepts the bill by signing it, thus converting it into a post-dated check and a binding contract.

Taxes and tariffs

Once they've landed at the dock or airport, the goods are taken to a warehouse and stored until they've passed a customs inspection.

What is this? Well, governments can make money from international trade. They do this by imposing duty, called a tariff or customs tax, on goods that enter their country.

Believe it or not, tariffs can also be used as a kind of weapon against another country. If country 'A' wants to damage country 'B' for some reason, it can apply such huge customs taxes that country 'B' can no longer sell at a reasonable price, and its export trade suffers.

What to pay

Customs tax

Customs officers are employed to check goods coming in and apply the correct tariff. There are two main types of tariff.

Specific tariffs are where a quantity of an item, such as a barrel of oil, is taxed regardless of its value.

An **"ad valorem"** tariff applies when a tax is calculated as a percentage of the assessed value of an item.

paying Duty

Every time you travel abroad – and when you return home – you will pass through customs. You may even be stopped and checked!

Customs officers check your luggage to make sure there's nothing in it that you need to pay customs duty, or tax, on. You're always allowed a certain amount of stuff tax-free. But you may have to pay tax on items like cameras, watches, and so on.

It's best to declare what you have to pay duty on. Not declaring it is an offense that will probably cost you more in fees than the item is worth.

Setting the Price

The price of anything is set by two things: the money it costs to make it and the price people will pay to own it. Some products are what is known as 'price sensitive.' These are goods that are necessities, like toothpaste, which people need but don't put a high value on. Others are luxuries where price often has nothing to do with cost.

SUPPLY AND DEMAND

Supply and demand describes the way a market works – how people decide the amount of a product that they are willing to buy.

If supply and demand are balanced, the number of people who want to buy will equal the amount of a product available to sell.

OVERLOAD!

However, if too many people want a product and its supply is limited or difficult to get hold of, then problems arise. The price may go up because the product is scarce. If the cost is too high, the demand of buyers will fall. Then, the seller will lose business and maybe fail.

The Right Price

So it's important to set the price correctly – to make sure it's the price people will pay to own it. The value of anything is the value someone is prepared to pay for it. But most items have a market value, too. This is based on what people have generally been prepared to pay for a similar item.

Price is always important. People have a limited amount of money to spend, and if they spend more on one thing, they cannot spend it on another. When the price of a product goes up, other competitive and cheaper products will sell better.

Haggling

Haggling is a way of getting the price reduced, and it's something everyone does. Of course, world traders don't 'haggle,' but they do negotiate. Everyone wants to pay the best price, so this often means putting in an offer which the seller can consider.

The seller may want a little more, the buyer offers a little more – slowly the price is established somewhere in the middle, and everyone should be happy.

GOLD

Gold is a precious metal. It is valued for its softness and its ductility, which means it can be drawn easily into fine wires without breaking. It's also very heavy. It weighs nineteen times as much as an equal volume of water. When most metals are heated they start to soften. But gold doesn't absorb heat easily, and therefore it holds its shape even when it's very hot.

Carat gold

Gold is measured in carats. This name came from an old measure that was the same as the weight of a carat, or carob seed.

Carat is now used to judge how pure the gold is. 24-carat gold is the purest kind of gold.

• • • • • • • • • •

Gold Standard

For thousands of years, gold was the standard of value; a base against which to measure currency. This helped countries trade with each other. A country was on the gold standard when it could convert its money into gold if required, and when it agreed to buy or sell gold at a fixed price. By 1900, all leading countries were using the gold standard to trade with each other.

GOLD RESERVES

Today most currency is based on the U.S. dollar as the standard, and not on the stocks of valuable gold bullion stored around the world. It is still a very valuable metal, but the enormous hoards of gold gathered by governments when gold was the most important measure now lie in storage.

Now, governments are rethinking their stockpiles. The central banks of the UK, Switzerland, the Netherlands, Belgium, Canada, Argentina, and Australia, have all sold significant stocks of gold.

The Mitsubishi gold bar.

Who's Storing What?

The largest gold reserves are held by the United States Treasury – approximately 147.3 million ounces of gold is being stored.

The biggest gold bar, weighing 551lb (250kg), was made by the Japanese company Mitsubishi Materials Corporation in December 1999. The gold is 99.99 percent pure. The bar measures 17.9 inches (45.5cm) wide and 8.9 inches (22.6 cm) long at the base and is 6.7 inches (17.0cm) tall.

Bank to Bank

Over the years, banks have played a large part in the spread of trade and industry around the world by making money available to merchants, manufacturers, and other institutions. Without their contribution, the world might be a very different place.

How banks started

Unfortunately for the early merchants, the world was not as safe a place as it is today. If they carried a load of money with them, they were in danger of being robbed.

But then, in northern Italy, a few noble families set up banks with agents in different cities. This allowed the merchants to deposit money in their home city in return for a letter of credit. The letter of credit could then be carried on their travels and exchanged for actual money in another place.

Another problem the merchants had was raising the huge sums of money needed to outfit ships as well as buy the goods to trade. Rather than use their own money, they got the banks to lend them the money for a share of the profit.

Bank investors

Today, many large banks have branches all over the world. They trade huge sums of money, investing in foreign currencies, in smaller businesses, and large corporations.

The financial center of Shanghai, China, has an impressive collection of towering banks and finance houses.

Banking is big

Every country in the world now has a banking center where companies carry out financial business. Some centers are larger and more influential than others, but banking is an important part of the business life of every country. Bankers make decisions that move huge sums of money around the world every second.

THE WORLD BANK

The World Bank is not a 'bank' in the real sense of the word. It's one of the agencies of the United Nations, and 184 different countries support it. These countries work together to make sure the Bank has money, and they also control how that money is spent. Together they have set up the World Bank to make sure that the poorer countries of the world get help when they need it.

FREE OF POVERTY

The mission of the World Bank states, 'Our dream is a world free of poverty.' We live in a world where the average person in some countries earns more than $40,000 a year. At the same time, the average person in some of the poorest countries only earns $700 a year. There is an enormous gap between these two figures. The poorest people on the planet not only suffer from food shortages, but they miss out on education, on health treatment, on water and electricity – on the basic necessities of life.

TO THE RESCUE

In response, the World Bank helps with loans and grants and with skilled people. The richest countries give billions of dollars each year to be spent on programs to help people in the poorest countries, to change their lives for the better.

At any one time, the Bank may have thousands of projects going on, and there are always new emergencies to meet. It sponsors many local projects, such as the installation of much-needed wells and water systems.

A new well brings fresh water to a village.

Orphan children are fed and educated at school.

New schools bring education to everyone.

Goods are dispatched from a charity warehouse.

iMF

IMF stands for International Monetary Fund, and while this is also not strictly a bank, it is an organization that collects and distributes huge sums of money.

But who does it lend this money to and why? Like the World Bank, the IMF is dedicated to helping countries around the world, but its work covers all countries, whether rich or poor. It wants to get everyone working and trading together for the benefit of all. If countries cooperate to trade with each other and grow their trade, the world will be more confident and stable.

The IMF aims:

* To promote international monetary and exchange stability.
* To help expand balanced growth of international trade.
* To help establish an easier system of payments between countries.

SHARING MONEY

A group of countries that cooperate and trade with each other, even to the point of sharing the same money, includes 19 of the countries in the European Union. They call themselves the Eurozone.

ECB

The European Central Bank, or ECB as it's known, is the central bank for Europe's single currency, the euro.

The euro is a new currency. It was introduced in 1999 in 12 separate countries of Europe, doing away with the French franc and Italian lira and German deutschmark and many others. Seven more countries have since adopted the euro.

The ECB's main task is to make sure that the euro is stable, which means watching prices everywhere to make sure one euro buys about the same amount of goods wherever it is used. So, if a cup of coffee costs 1 euro in France, it should be about the same price everywhere else, too.

Sharing the euro⍟

Nineteen countries share the euro:

* Austria
* Belgium
* Cyprus
* Estonia
* Finland
* France
* Germany
* Greece
* Ireland
* Italy
* Latvia
* Lithuania
* Luxembourg
* Malta
* The Netherlands
* Portugal
* Slovenia
* Slovakia
* Spain

A single currency

What does it mean to share your money with other countries, most of whom speak a different language, are thousands of miles away, and who live their lives and go about their work in a different way, too?

It has proved a lot more difficult than many thought back in 1999.

The new headquarters of the European Bank under construction. It opened in 2015.

Does Euro-sharing work?

Yes

* Trade is made much easier because it removes the need to exchange money.
* The risk of different currencies losing value is removed.
* A citizen of Europe can find the best price for a product from any euro country.
* Labor and goods can flow more easily between countries.
* Money is managed by the ECB, so it is not influenced by a specific government.

No

* The system is more in favor of the larger euro countries than the smaller ones.
* If countries get into too much debt then they can cause problems for other countries in the system.
* A strong euro can make goods more expensive to buy and also threaten exports.

World Wealth

As well as rich people, there are also rich countries. These usually become wealthy because of the trade that they do with other countries, perhaps selling raw materials such as iron and timber, or even the particular skills of their people.

GDP

The world's richest nations are measured by how much each person living in the country contributes to its overall wealth – or earns – in any year. It's called the Gross Domestic Product or GDP.

The Richest:
* Australia
* Austria
* Brunei
* Canada
* Denmark
* Germany
* Hong Kong
* Iceland
* Ireland
* Kuwait
* Luxembourg
* Netherlands
* Norway
* Qatar
* Singapore
* Sweden
* Switzerland
* Taiwan
* United Arab Emirate (UAE)
* United States

* *Gross Domestic Product Based on Purchasing-Power-Parity (PPP) Per Capita*

The U.S., Argentina, and Australia have large land areas where cattle are raised and exported worldwide as meat.

South Korea has a large shipbuilding industry. It sells its ships worldwide.

Qatar, Brunei, UAE, and Kuwait have oil to export worldwide.

Cost of living

Some countries may be wealthy, but they are also very expensive to live in. They have what is known as a high cost of living.

If you want to make money and live cheaply, these are some places to avoid:

* Japan
* South Korea
* Russia
* Taiwan
* Norway
* Hong Kong
* Switzerland
* Denmark
* Argentina
* China

G7

The G7 is a term used to describe the seven most advanced business and industrial countries in the world.

WORKING together

The purpose of the G7 is to discuss, and possibly to influence, economic and political situations in the world through an annual summit meeting as well as various other policy meetings and research gatherings. The location of the meeting alternates each year among the member states.

* Canada
* France
* Germany
* Italy
* Japan
* United Kingdom
* United States

Recently, the annual meetings have been the focus of protests against large corporations who are seen as growing too fast at others' expense. The member countries are sometimes seen to be more interested in increasing their own wealth than in helping poorer countries increase theirs. However, they do agree on large issues such as world peace, and work together to resolve conflicts.

Rising giants

Perhaps the G7 membership is out of date!
New rich countries are emerging. China
contributes significantly more to global
growth than all member countries of Europe
combined. And India isn't far behind China.
The world economy is shifting, and the biggest
players are not part of the G7.

Speeding up

Things continue to change all the time. When
richer countries run into problems, their
economies can slow down to a standstill – or
even worse! (See light blue and pale yellow on the chart below.) Meanwhile,
poorer countries – many in Africa, South America, and Asia – benefit from
investment and money gifts, or aid, and start to grow – fast! (See orange
and red on the chart.)

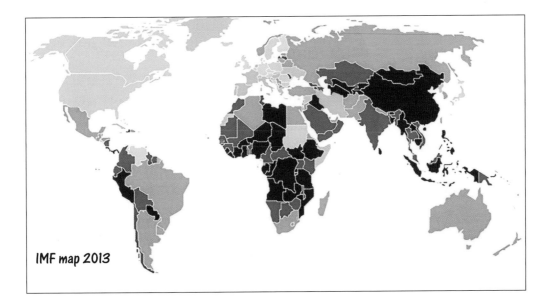

IMF map 2013

World Poverty

Just like people, whole countries can be considered
poor. A poor country is one that has a low GDP per
person, one that has few natural resources, or one
that doesn't export many goods to make money.
The reasons behind the poverty can be put down
to natural causes, such as the weather, soil makeup,
or geography. It's difficult to grow enough to feed
the population or sell abroad if the land is desert.
Or perhaps there aren't any rich minerals or metals
or oil to be mined and sold.

Millions in Poverty

Poverty means not being able to contribute
to the society in which you live. It means
suffering shortages, illiteracy, and poor health.
It means living in areas that take the brunt of
environmental damage, such as busy, congested
roads, factories, and even waste dumps. You may
even need to use the dump to find food, or
objects to sell for a living!

And it means living with little
self-respect or hope for the future.

The Poorest

* Afghanistan
* Burundi
* Central African
     Republic
* Comoros
* Congo - Kinshasa
* Eritrea
* Ethiopia
* Guinea
* Guinea-Bissau
* Haiti
* Liberia
* Madagascar
* Malawi
* Mali
* Mozambique
* Nepal
* Niger
* South Sudan
* Togo
* Zimbabwe

Why Poor?

There are many reasons why some countries are poor. Climate may play a part. Often, both climate conditions and unexpected natural disasters contribute to poverty. Some cities hold too many people, and many cannot find work or a home.

Homes made of scraps are put together on wasteland.

Slums such as these breed disease and sickness.

No Resources

There may be few natural resources a country can use to either develop its own economy or to sell abroad as exports. Or it may not have easy access to foreign markets. In many poor countries, there's no history of modern industry, the kind that has created wealth for the industrialized countries of the world. Also, some of the poor countries have been dependent on commodities that have dropped in value.

1.2 billion people on our planet are trying to live on less than a dollar a day.

Helping Each Other

One thing that has not helped the poor countries is debt. Many of them have borrowed money from rich countries over the years to help feed their people – even to help pay for their wars.

Third World Debt

We all know what it means to have a personal debt we can't repay – even if it's just to our mom! But what if it's a country that's borrowed the money and can't pay back the debt?

The World Bank and The IMF began to identify countries that were in severe debt. These countries are sometimes called HIPCs, which means Heavily Indebted Poor Countries. Many had debts that were so great that they could not pay all the interest on them – let alone pay back the debt itself.

And to make matters worse, debt repayment was using up the money that could be better spent on health, education, and building.

Canceling Debts

Something had to be done. Everyone finally agreed that poor countries needed to get rid of their debt burdens, and that these should simply be written off and forgotten.

NO Debt SUCCESSES

To qualify to have debts canceled, the countries had to use the money they would have used to repay their debts on programs that would get rid of hunger and poverty instead.

As of 2012, 36 of the 39 countries identified as HIPCs had worked with the World Bank and IMF to reduce or eliminate their debts.

AiD helps

Some countries have been even more successful. The top ten fastest growing countries in the world have included Angola, Myanmar, Ethiopia, Cambodia, Nigeria, and Rwanda – all currently large aid recipients. The World Bank blog states that most of today's stable low-income countries could reach middle-income status by 2025.

A small amount of cash helps farmers plant and harvest surplus crops for sale.

GiVe knowleDge

Maybe there will be fewer loans to poor countries. Now it is accepted that helping with knowledge, education, and skills training is probably more useful than cash.

FAIR TRADE

For many years, the richer countries have produced more food than they need. But rather than tell their farmers to produce less, they have insisted that the poorer countries take their surplus mountains of sugar, wheat, rice, and so on – at bargain prices.

Handouts

Now this sounds as if it might be helpful. But of course, it hasn't been helpful at all! The imported food was priced cheaper than the local produce. So while some rich country's farmers were getting rid of their surplus stock – AND getting paid for it – the farmers in the poorer countries were losing business and money!

The symbol of the Fair Trade organization

It's not Fair!

To help reduce this problem, some smaller companies have helped to set up a system called Fair Trade, where the farmer or other supplier is paid a fair amount for the goods they supply.

Fair and green

Do you think about what you are buying? Are you a 'green shopper'?

Like Fair Trade, green buying takes us back to ethics. It's about purchasing stuff that's healthy or that doesn't require destroying an entire rainforest in South America. Working together with millions of others, everyone of us can help have a huge impact on the environment. Although we don't always see the effects, everything we buy comes from the Earth and returns to it in one form or another.

Banana growers work together to make Fair Trade agreements with buyers worldwide.

Green buying

Green buying isn't always easy because you may have to pay a bit more for your items and because outlets are hard to find. But if you buy stuff that's better for the planet, you will be joining many millions of people who want to make a difference.

DISASTER!

Unfortunately, any country can be hit by some kind of disaster from time to time. This may be a flood, earthquake, or even a war. Such disasters quickly have an effect on business and trade – and on a country's ability to function properly.

DROUGHT ...

Unfortunately, no one can do much about a natural disaster until after it's happened. Many parts of northern and central Africa have a history of drought. The only difference is that these droughts are now happening every 5 years instead of every 10 to 15, and they are more severe than ever. Droughts bring crop failure and hunger to the people.

... and hunger

Other factors contribute to famine as well, including a high population growth rate, smaller farm sizes, poor farming techniques, deforestation, and poor soil.

FOOD help

Given the size of the problem, it's easy to see why a natural disaster such as drought can cause terrible suffering. Many countries still depend on food aid to feed millions of their people.

WARS

When a war breaks out, either between countries or between groups within countries, millions of dollars are spent on soldiers and military equipment that could have been used to buy food. It is estimated that millions of dollars a day are spent on fighting wars around the world.

Apart from the pain and terror and upheaval to people's lives, wars take up manpower and resources that could be better used to build a country's economy and raise everyone's standard of living.

It takes resources to fight a war.

Refugees from wars living in makeshift camps.

What's Best for Us?

The World Bank has normally judged the wealth of its 180+ member countries around the world by their money wealth. But now it measures things like education provision, human rights records, and life-expectancy, as well as cultural values and activities for self-improvement and group participation.

GNH not GDP

In the kingdom of Bhutan, a mountainous country high in the Himalayan mountains, they go even further. Here a ruler, King Jigme Singye Wangchuck, believed that happiness is more important than wealth. Bhutan is the only country in the world to measure its well-being by Gross National Happiness (GNH).

PRIORITY

Most countries worry about their ability to buy and sell things, and whether they can afford all the things they need and want. But not Bhutan! King Wangchuck thought that if his country tried to develop in line with other countries, it would need to sacrifice its old-fashioned traditions, its heritage and culture, and its beautiful mountain environment. In Bhutan, happiness really does take priority over economic wealth.

The Value ✦ of a simple life

In some religions, happiness is not decided by what we have and own - although this can be useful in reducing poverty and encouraging people's generosity - but by our knowledge, our imagination, and our living skills.

Gandhi

A statue of Mohandas Gandhi

Mohandas Gandhi was a Hindu lawyer who helped India become an independent nation. He was a great politician and thinker, but he also became a symbol of simple values. He believed that living a simple life would bring more happiness than seeking financial wealth.

United World

Working together

We'd all like to see a stable world where everyone has an opportunity to make the best of their life regardless of what background they come from. Unfortunately, poverty exists everywhere. Hundreds of millions of people live in poverty, even in the richest nations of the world.

It seems incredible that in a world where there's so much wealth and so much money, that anyone should be poor at all. Institutions such as the IMF try to do what they can to create a more balanced world. But it isn't easy.

can you help?

You may think that in this vast world of ours, most things happen without your being able to influence them. So it's easy to shrug and say there's nothing you can do. But just being aware of what is going on around the world is an important start.

Things That Help ...

Contributing to charities helps – especially when there is some disaster. Lives may be changed by even the smallest donation. If you don't buy products made with child labor, you might just help to stop this practice. And looking for the Fair Trade sign on food helps traders who need it.

Money isn't everything

Money makes the world go 'round, that's true, but there are other things that can and do count and that are just as important.

Let's Discuss This!

ARE quotas good or bad?

Sometimes countries limit the amount of a certain product they will import. This is to protect industries or areas of high employment. Do you think this is fair? Can you see how this might not work as planned? Research and find out what industries near you would be impacted by quotas – both imported or exported.

Should the G7 accept more members?

The authors state that the G7 excludes some large economic countries and should consider adding them. Find out why the G7 has not added these members and if you think these reasons make sense.

What is success?

Should the success of a nation be judged by its ability to produce and consume, or should it be based on the quality of life in that country, or the happiness of its people? Should we put more value on things such as fresh water, green forests, clean air, and traditional ways of life? If a country makes money from cutting down logs, should it somehow factor in the loss of the forest?

is EURO-sharing a good idea?

The pros and cons of countries sharing the euro are listed on page 42. Do you think the euro is a good idea and that it is working, or do you think countries should have their own currency? Research articles in the news to get more information and get the point of view of rich and poor countries within the Eurozone.

Additional Resources

B☆☮☆KS

Anniss, Matt. *World Economics: What's the Future?* New York, New York: Gareth Stevens, 2013.

Dicker, Katie. *The True Cost of Food: How to Shop to Change the World.* New York, New York: Crabtree Publishing, 2014.

Hollander, Barbara. *How the World Bank and International Monetary Fund Work.* New York, New York: Rosen Publishing Company, 2013.

• •

Websites

Factmonster
www.factmonster.com/ipka/A0769539.html
This site provides information about countries around the world and their currency.

Youngzine
www.youngzine.org/all/world-news
Learn about current events and conditions in the world.

Glossary

aid
Money, as well as foods, medicines, or other supplies, that are often sent to poorer countries who need them.

balance of payments
The difference between the amount of money a country receives from exports, and the amount it spends on imports.

brand
A mark or name on a manufacturer's products that is easily recognized.

charity
An organization that provides money or help to people who need it.

commodities
The name given to essential products, such as grains and metals, that are bought and sold in large quantities around the world.

debt
Borrowed money to be repaid.

economy
The system of trade and industry by which the wealth of a country is made and used.

export
The sale of goods to other countries.

Fair Trade
A system where buyers and sellers agree a fair and just price for their goods. Fair Trade goods are labeled in the stores.

government
The group of people installed or elected to run a country on behalf of its people.

import
To buy goods and services from a foreign country.

market value
The price that something could be sold for at a particular time.

merchant
A person or business that buys and sells products in large amounts for profit, often trading with other countries.

poverty
The state of not having enough money for basic needs.

price
The cost of buying something that usually reflects the cost of making it as well as what people will pay for it.

specialization
A special area of production where a country can succeed and export.

supply and demand
The idea that the price of something depends on how much there is available and how many people want to buy it.

tariff
A tax imposed on imported goods and services to restrict trade by increasing the price.

trade gap
A situation in which the value of a country's imports is greater than the value of goods it exports.

Index